ECCLESIASTES
& SONG OF SONGS

THEOLOGY OF WORK PROJECT

ECCLESIASTES & SONG OF SONGS

THE BIBLE AND YOUR WORK
Study Series

HENDRICKSON
PUBLISHERS

Theology of Work
The Bible and Your Work Study Series:
Ecclesiastes & Song of Songs

© 2016 by Hendrickson Publishers Marketing, LLC
P.O. Box 3473
Peabody, Massachusetts 01961-3473

ISBN 978-1-61970-757-3

William Messenger, Executive Editor, Theology of Work Project
Sean McDonough, Biblical Editor, Theology of Work Project
Patricia Anders, Editorial Director, Hendrickson Publishers

Contributors:

Christopher Gilbert, "Ecclesiastes and Song of Songs" Bible Study
Duane Garrett, "Ecclesiastes and Work" and "Song of Songs and Work" in the *Theology of Work Bible Commentary*

The Theology of Work Project is an independent, international organization dedicated to researching, writing, and distributing materials with a biblical perspective on work. The Project's primary mission is to produce resources covering every book of the Bible plus major topics in today's workplaces. Wherever possible, the Project collaborates with other faith-and-work organizations, churches, universities and seminaries to help equip people for meaningful, productive work of every kind.

Printed in the United States of America

First Printing—April 2016

Contents

The Theology of Work

Work is not only a human calling, but also a divine one. "In the beginning God created the heavens and the earth." God worked to create us and created us to work. "The LORD God took the man and put him in the garden of Eden to till it and keep it" (Gen. 2:15). God also created work to be good, even if it's hard to see in a fallen world. To this day, God calls us to work to support ourselves and to serve others (Eph. 4:28).

Work can accomplish many of God's purposes for our lives—the basic necessities of food and shelter, as well as a sense of fulfillment and joy. Our work can create ways to help people thrive; it can discover the depths of God's creation; and it can bring us into wonderful relationships with co-workers and those who benefit from our work (customers, clients, patients, and so forth).

Yet many people face drudgery, boredom, or exploitation at work. We have bad bosses, hostile relationships, and unfriendly work environments. Our work seems useless, unappreciated, faulty, frustrating. We don't get paid enough. We get stuck in dead-end jobs or laid off or fired. We fail. Our skills become obsolete. It's a struggle just to make ends meet. But how can this be if God created work to be good—and what can we do about it? God's answers for these questions must be somewhere in the Bible, but where?

The Theology of Work Project's mission has been to study what the Bible says about work and to develop resources to apply the

Christian faith to our work. It turns out that every book of the Bible gives practical, relevant guidance that can help us do our jobs better, improve our relationships at work, support ourselves, serve others more effectively, and find meaning and value in our work. The Bible shows us how to live all of life—including work—in Christ. Only in Jesus can we and our work be transformed to become the blessing it was always meant to be.

To put it another way, if we are not following Christ during the 100,000 hours of our lives that we spend at work, are we really following Christ? Our lives are more than just one day a week at church. The fact is that God cares about our life *every day of the week*. But how do we become equipped to follow Jesus at work? In the same ways we become equipped for every aspect of life in Christ—listening to sermons, modeling our lives on others' examples, praying for God's guidance, and most of all by studying the Bible and putting it into practice.

This Theology of Work series contains a variety of books to help you apply the Scriptures and Christian faith to your work. This Bible study is one volume in the series The Bible and Your Work. It is intended for those who want to explore what the Bible says about work and how to apply it to their work in positive, practical ways. Although it can be used for individual study, Bible study is especially effective with a group of people committed to practicing what they read in Scripture. In this way, we gain from one another's perspectives and are encouraged to actually *do* what we read in Scripture. Because of the direct focus on work, The Bible and Your Work studies are especially suited for Bible studies *at* work or *with* other people in similar occupations. The following lessons are designed for thirty-minute lunch breaks (or perhaps breakfast before work) during a five-day work week.

Christians today recognize God's calling to us in and through our work—for ourselves and for those whom we serve. May God use this book to help you follow Christ in every sphere of life and work.

Will Messenger, Executive Editor
Theology of Work Project

Chapter 1

Ecclesiastes and Work

(Ecclesiastes 1)

Lesson #1: Introduction to Ecclesiastes

Like a mirror to our contemporary world, Ecclesiastes captures the poignancy of toil and joy, fleeting success, and unanswered questions arising in our daily round of work. For many of us, its unvarnished assessment of the human condition makes it a favorite book and its narrator—called the Teacher or Preacher—has a lot to say about work.

Most of us spend the largest portion of our waking lives working, and we find affirmation when the Teacher says, "I commend enjoyment, for there is nothing better for people under the sun than to eat, and drink, and enjoy themselves, for this will go with them in their toil through the days of life that God gives them under the sun" (Eccl. 8:15).

Yet the Teacher's picture of work is also deeply troubling. A deluge of negative observations about work threatens to overwhelm the reader. He opens with "vanity of vanities" (Eccl. 1:2) and ends with "all is vanity" (Eccl. 12:10). The words and phrases he repeats most often are "vanity," "a chasing after wind," "not find out," and "can't find out." Without a larger perspective to temper his observations, Ecclesiastes can be very disheartening to readers.

 *Food for Thought*

If you have read Ecclesiastes previously, what have you already gained from it? If this is your first time reading it, what is your immediate impression? What do you think is the writer's purpose?

_____

_____

_____

_____

_____

_____

_____

We could read Ecclesiastes as simply a tossed salad of observations about life and work. By this approach, the Teacher is a realist who reports the ups and downs of life. Each observation stands as its own wisdom. If we draw useful advice from, say, "There is nothing better for mortals than to eat and drink, and find enjoyment in their toil" (Eccl. 2:24), then we won't be concerned that it is followed shortly by, "This also is vanity and a chasing after wind" (Eccl. 2:26). Most contemporary scholars don't recognize an overarching argument in Ecclesiastes, and among those who do, there are few who agree on what that is. Yet we can't help wanting to know the overall message of Ecclesiastes.

One scholar, Addison Wright, divides the book into units of thought. Wright's structure commends itself for three reasons: (1) It is based objectively on the repetition of key phrases, not subjective interpretations of the content; (2) it is accepted by more scholars than any other (among those who accept *any* overall structure); and (3) it brings work-related topics to the foreground.

 Food for Thought

From your reading of Ecclesiastes, which way do you lean in interpreting its meaning? Are you satisfied with a tossed salad approach? Or are you unsatisfied and looking for an overarching purpose? Why?

_____

_____

_____

_____

_____

_____

_____

This study focuses on the repetitive phrases that highlight Wright's idea. In the first half of the book, the phrase "a chasing after wind" marks the end of each unit. In the second half, the phrase "not find out" (or "who can find out?") does the same. Throughout the book, we read "under the sun," which occurs twenty-nine times in Ecclesiastes but nowhere else in the Bible. It is like the term "in the fallen world," derived from Genesis 3, which describes the world as one where God's creation is still good yet severely marred by ills.

Does the Teacher mean to reinforce the pointlessness of work by conjuring an image of the sun circling endlessly across the sky while nothing ever changes? Or does he imagine there might be a world beyond the Fall, not "under the sun," where work would not be in vain? Keep these questions in mind as we read Ecclesiastes!

In contrast to human life "under the sun," the Teacher gives us glimpses of God in heaven. Our toil is fleeting, but "whatever God does endures forever" (Eccl. 3:14). We will consider what Ecclesiastes reveals about God's character as aspects like this arise, and then review them toward the end of our study.

In this way, you will discover anew the refreshing honesty of Ecclesiastes, and how it encourages conversation about work beyond simplistic prescriptions for living God's way. At the end of the study, we will look at how Ecclesiastes relates to the good news of Christ.

 Food for Thought

How open do you think you might be to the insights of an apparently pessimistic "Teacher"? What do you hope to gain from this study? Write your answers down for reference at the end.

_____

_____

_____

_____

_____

_____

Prayer

Pause for a few moments of silence to reflect on this lesson. Then offer a prayer, either spontaneous or by using the following:

Lord,

We sit in daily tension between a temporary life "under the sun" and belief in your promises of eternal life. Grant that we might begin this study with hearts open to receive the pointed truths of the Teacher in order to serve your purposes in our working lives more gladly.

Amen.

Lesson #2: Endless, Meaningless Work? (Ecclesiastes 1:1–11)

"What do people gain from all the toil at which they toil under the sun?" (Eccl. 1:3)

Work is central to the observations in Ecclesiastes. It is generally called "toil" (Hebrew, *amal*), which indicates its hardship. The Teacher's assessment of toil is that it is "vanity" (Eccl. 2:1). This word, *hebel* in Hebrew, is like the drumbeat of the book. *Hebel* actually means "breath," and as a metaphor it has a double meaning and is superbly suited as the keyword for this book. A breath is by nature brief and of little discernible substance, quickly dissipating. Yet our survival hangs upon these brief intakes and exhalations of air. Soon enough, however, breathing will cease and life will end. So *hebel* describes something of fleeting value that will ultimately come to an end.

"Vanity" is in some ways an inadequate translation, since it appears to assert that everything is utterly pointless and of no value, whereas *hebel* suggests more profoundly that something has a fleeting, ephemeral value. A single breath may not have permanent value, but in its one moment it keeps us alive. In the same way, what we are and do in this transitory life has real, though temporary, significance.

 Food for Thought

Consider the use of the word *hebel*. How does this change the way you read Ecclesiastes? In what way is the translation "vanity" a help or hindrance to grasping the meaning of the author?

_____

_____

_____

_____

_____

_____

Consider shipbuilding. By God's good creation, the earth holds the raw materials we need to build ships. Human ingenuity and hard work—also created by God—can make safe, capable, even beautiful ships. They transport food, resources, manufactured goods, and people to wherever they are needed.

When a ship is launched and the bottle of champagne broken across its bow, all those involved celebrate their accomplishment. Yet once it leaves the yard, the builders lose control over it. It may be captained by a fool who wrecks it on a reef. It may be chartered to smuggle drugs, weapons, or even slaves. Its crew may be treated harshly. It may serve nobly for many years, yet even so it will wear out and become obsolete.

Its eventual fate is a shipbreaking yard or beach. It passes, like the puffs of wind that once powered ships, first into rusty bones, then into a mix of recycled metal and discarded waste, and finally is forgotten altogether. Ships are good, but they do not last forever. As long as we live, we also work in this tension.

 Food for Thought

Consider your own work. What is the likely outcome of the products or services you provide? How lasting will they be, and how does that realization sit with you? In facing the temporariness of work, where do you find your satisfaction in it?

_____

_____

_____

_____

_____

_____

_____

This brings us to the image of the sun arcing around the earth (Eccl. 1:5). The ceaseless activity by this great light in the sky brings visibility and the warmth we depend on every day, yet it changes nothing as the ages go by: "There is nothing new under the sun" (Eccl. 1:9).

It is interesting to read historical biographies of politicians, such as *John Adams* by David McCullough, if only to marvel that the nature of politics, like the nature of its changing cast of characters, has not changed much (if at all) in over two hundred years. And yet there is a resonance to truth found in Shakespearean plays even four hundred years after their advent, because their plot lines have been enacted in the real events of human history and in so many diverse contexts before and since.

So with great acuity of wisdom, the Teacher provides us with his unsentimental observation, "There is nothing new under the sun," which is nonetheless *not* an eternal condemnation of our work.

 Food for Thought

Is this a fair observation by the Teacher? Explain how you would defend or deny the statement "There is nothing new under the sun" from your work experience or your understanding of the history of your field of work. How does it affect the way you work?

_____

_____

_____

_____

_____

_____

_____

Prayer

Pause for a few moments of silence to reflect on this lesson. Then offer a prayer, either spontaneous or by using the following:

Lord,

Daily we face the repeating cycles of human achievement and failure, which seem so relentless—until we remember that you entered history and changed the trajectory of human life, a change to which we are witnesses. Help us to face the work at which we toil with hearts and minds open for ways to reflect this.

Amen.

Chapter 2

A Chasing after Wind?

(Ecclesiastes 2–5)

Lesson #1: Achievement and Pleasure

In Ecclesiastes 1:1–11, the Teacher declared his theme that toil is "vanity," or at least ephemeral. Now he explores seven possibilities for living life well. He considers achievement, pleasure, wisdom, wealth, timing, friendship, and finding joy in God's gifts. In some of these he does find a certain value, lesser in the earlier explorations and greater in the latter. Yet nothing seems permanent, and the characteristic conclusion in each section is that work comes to "a chasing after wind." In this lesson, we will consider the first two of these possibilities: work with the goal of achievement and work with the goal of pleasure.

 Food for Thought

Consider the list of goals that the Teacher said he pursued in his work. Which of these do you believe are legitimate goals for work and which illusory? Why?

_____

_____

_____

_____

Achievement (Ecclesiastes 1:12–18)

The teacher was both a king and a sage—perhaps an overachiever by modern assessment—"surpassing all who were over Jerusalem before me" (Eccl. 1:16). And what did all his achievement mean to him? "It is an unhappy business that God has given to human beings to be busy with. I saw all the deeds that are done under the sun; and see, all is vanity and a chasing after wind" (Eccl. 1:13–14).

No lasting achievement even seems possible. "What is crooked cannot be made straight, and what is lacking cannot be counted" (Eccl. 1:15). Achieving his goals did not give him happiness, for it only made him realize how hollow and limited anything he could accomplish must be. In sum, he says again, "I perceived that this also is but a chasing after wind" (Eccl. 1:17–18).

 Food for Thought

Make a short list of your achievements or the achievements you see in the lives of others. What did the Teacher say about such achievements? What merit is there in his conclusions?

Pleasure (Ecclesiastes 2:1–11)

Next he says, "Come now, I will make a test of pleasure; enjoy yourself" (Eccl. 2:1). He acquires wealth, houses, gardens, alcohol, servants (slaves), jewelry, entertainment, and ready access to sexual pleasure. "Whatever my eyes desired I did not keep from them; I kept my heart from no pleasure" (Eccl. 2:10a). Unlike the goal of achievement, he finds some value in seeking pleasure. "My heart found pleasure in all my toil, and this was my reward for all my toil" (Eccl. 2:10b). His supposed achievements were never unique or lasting, but his pleasures at least were pleasurable.

It seems that work undertaken as a means to an end—in this case, pleasure—is more satisfying than work undertaken as an obsession. Today's workers might do well to take the time to smell the roses in their daily routine. If we have ceased to work toward a goal beyond work, if we can no longer enjoy the fruits of our labor, then we have become slaves of work rather than its masters.

Nonetheless, he comes to regard toiling merely in order to gain pleasure as ultimately unsatisfying: "Again, all was vanity and a chasing after wind, and there was nothing to be gained under the sun" (Eccl. 2:11).

 Food for Thought

What do you make of the Teacher's argument here? Is there something to be gained by seeking some pleasure from your work, different from achievement for the sake of achievement? If so, what is that for you? Why then do you think the Teacher concludes that even his enjoyment of pleasure provided by his work is a vanity?

_____

_____

_____

_____

Prayer

Pause for a few moments of silence to reflect on this lesson. Then offer a prayer, either spontaneous or by using the following:

Lord,

Help us to know what is worth achieving and what pleasures are valid as we go about our work. Make us clear-eyed about what can be achieved and enjoyed so we can find the meaning you intend for us in our work.

Amen.

Lesson #2: Wisdom and Wealth

Wisdom (Ecclesiastes 2:12–26)

You may have noticed that television advertising promotes not so much the virtues of the product itself as the reasons that you must have it. These may range from a feeling of joy to belonging to the cool crowd, and even to attracting a sexual partner.

The Teacher gets the same idea in regard to his work. Perhaps it will be good to seek an object beyond the work itself, and so he shoots for an objective higher than mere pleasure, namely wisdom. "I turned to consider wisdom and madness and folly" (Eccl. 2:12). In order to work for knowledge and wisdom he becomes something like a professor or researcher. Unlike achievement for achievement's sake, wisdom can at least be attained as a lasting asset to some degree. "I saw that wisdom excels folly as light excels darkness" (Eccl. 2:13). But despite the depth and breadth of understanding it brings to a person's mind, even for the good of others, he still realizes that it makes no difference ultimately, "for the wise die just like fools" (Eccl. 1:16).

Professors are as much prone to accident, disease, and other misfortune as other people, so what is the lasting advantage of wisdom? In the case of the Teacher, pursuing wisdom led him to the brink of despair (Eccl. 1:17)—something many people feel who have tried to master a specific field of knowledge! And so, the Teacher concludes in regard to that effort, "All is vanity and a chasing after wind" (Eccl. 2:17).

 Food for Thought

Consider your immediate response to the Teacher's words in regard to scholarship. Do you agree or not? Explain why or why not. Why does the Teacher press this point?

_____

_____

_____

_____

_____

_____

Wealth (Ecclesiastes 2:18–26)

The Teacher now turns to accumulating wealth as a goal beyond the work itself. But the result seems worse than spending wealth to gain pleasure, because wealth brings with it the problem of inheritance. When people die, their wealth passes to someone who may be completely undeserving. "Sometimes one who has toiled with wisdom and knowledge and skill must leave all to be enjoyed by another who did not toil for it. This also is vanity and a great evil" (Eccl. 2:21). This is *so* galling that the Teacher says, "I turned and gave my heart up to despair" (Eccl. 2:20).

Many who accumulate great wealth find it extremely unsatisfying. No matter how much we gain, it never seems to be enough. But as age or experience sharpens the sense our mortality, giving away our wealth wisely can be an intolerable burden. In the United States, this burden has spawned many philanthropic foundations that outlive their founders. Andrew Carnegie once said, "I resolved to stop accumulating and begin the infinitely more serious and difficult task of wise distribution." And because God is a giver, it should be no surprise that the distribution of wealth, rather than its accumulation, might be the more satisfying project.

 Food for Thought

Consider someone whose struggle with wealth makes regular headlines. How would you describe that person's burden? How do you regard accumulating money in your own life?

_____

_____

_____

_____

_____

_____

It is interesting that we get our first glimpse here of the character of God. God is a giver, and "to the one who pleases him God gives wisdom and knowledge and joy" (Eccl. 2:26). This aspect of God's character is repeated several times through his gifts of food, drink, and joy (Eccl. 5:18, 8:15), wealth and possessions (Eccl. 5:19, 6:20), honor (Eccl. 6:2), integrity (Eccl. 7:29), the world we inhabit (Eccl. 11:5), and life itself (Eccl. 12:7).

But the Teacher does not find satisfaction in giving wealth any more than in gaining it (Eccl. 2:18–21). The satisfaction God *in heaven* finds in giving somehow escapes the Teacher "under the sun." He does not seem to consider the possibility of investing wealth or giving it away for a higher purpose. Unless there is indeed a higher purpose beyond anything the Teacher discovers, the accumulation and distribution of wealth "also is vanity and a chasing after wind" (Eccl. 2:26).

 Food for Thought

Does the Teacher suggest it is pointless to establish foundations or to build up educational or hospital endowments? What kinds of investments do you think we can make with our wealth that might give our work satisfying meaning and purpose? Or is it better to spend or give away everything you have before you die?

_____

_____

_____

_____

_____

_____

Prayer

Pause for a few moments of silence to reflect on this lesson. Then offer a prayer, either spontaneous or by using the following:

> *Lord,*
>
> *We acknowledge that you are indeed the giver of life and breath to each of us, and all the good things in our short lives. Help us to discover your purpose for whatever wealth we accumulate through our work and to put our wealth at your disposal.*
>
> *Amen.*

Lesson #3: Timing (Ecclesiastes 3:1–4:6)

Since the teacher concludes that work has no single unchanging purpose, he next explores the possibility of multiple purposes, each meaningful in its own moment. "For everything there is a season, and a time for every matter under heaven" (Eccl. 3:1). Every activity is governed by *time*. Like the animals, we are creatures of time; yet unlike them, we have "a sense of past and future" in our minds, giving us a hint of eternity (Eccl. 3:11). If we are smart about doing the right thing at the right time, perhaps the events of our lives build on one another and create something with lasting value.

Marketers strive to find the right time to release products—a time when the winds of human desire are at their most favorable. You would stock the shelves if a sports team won a major championship, but you probably wouldn't if they had lost, and car manufacturers frequently offer special deals to coincide with national holidays. Meanwhile, manufacturers pursue just-in-time inventory control to reduce costs and increase quality.

Work that is necessary at one moment can be inappropriate at another. Dancing would be a fool's choice during a courtroom trial, but has its proper place at an inaugural ball. Timing often dictates the success or failure of business ventures. "I was born at the right place and time," Bill Gates remarked about his amazing success at Microsoft. "Our timing in setting up the first software company aimed at personal computers was essential to our success." Microsoft happened to have developed its microcomputer operating system just at the moment IBM was looking for an operating system for a new product it called the "personal computer." Yet, while timing is everything in business "under the sun," it is often beyond our ability to anticipate.

 Food for Thought

Consider the products or services your work delivers. List the ways in which getting the timing right governs what you do. Give examples from your work experience of when timing was done well and when it wasn't. Is good timing a good recipe for finding meaning in work?

Good timing is better than poor timing. Yet we deceive ourselves about the fundamental nature of life if we think our labors can effect permanent peace, prosperity, or happiness. Even well-maintained cars take their final drives to the scrap yard. Bridges rust and need constant maintenance and eventual replacement. Everything we build will eventually be torn down (Eccl. 3:3). Rapidly evolving technologies amplify the need for us to adapt and change our work tools and practices, or even force us into a succession of newly conceived jobs. And more than twenty-five hundred years ago, the Teacher found no sign of eternally significant work "under the sun" (Eccl. 4:1).

Even if we manage to do the right thing at the right time, the good we try to do may be thwarted by people with bad intentions. "On the side of their oppressors there was power—with no one to comfort them" (Eccl. 4:1). Whoever has the greatest power has the greatest ability to oppress. Thus oppression is at its worst when it comes from governments and law enforcement, as all those who struggle for human and civil rights have experienced. "I saw under the sun that in the place of justice, wickedness was there" (Eccl. 3:16).

Yet the powerless are not necessarily better people, for they are prone to envy. We envy those who have the power, wealth, status, relationships, possessions, or other things we lack. The Teacher recognizes that envy is as bad as oppression. "I saw that all toil and skill in work come from one person's envy of another. This also is vanity and a chasing after wind" (Eccl. 4:4). The drive to gain achievement, pleasure, wisdom, or wealth either by oppression or because of envy is an utter waste of time. Yet who has never fallen into these follies?

 *Food for Thought*

To what degree do you think the human condition is frustrated or freed by having the capacity to live beyond our moment in time? And to what degree do you see your workplace affected by the misuse of power or envy of the powerful? What are the outcomes you have observed?

_____

_____

_____

_____

_____

_____

_____

_____

But the Teacher does not despair. "God has made everything suitable for its time" (Eccl. 3:11a). It is right to cry at the funeral of a loved one, and it is good to rejoice at the birth of a child. And we should not refuse the legitimate pleasures our work may bring. "There is nothing better for them than to be happy and enjoy themselves as long as they live; moreover, it is God's gift that all should eat and drink and take pleasure in all their toil" (Eccl. 3:12–13).

To underline this application to our work he says, "So I saw that there is nothing better than that all should enjoy their work, for that is their lot" (Eccl. 3:22a). Work suffers from the curse, but work is not a curse. (For more on this, see *Genesis 1–11* in The Theology of Work Bible and Your Work Study Series.) Even the limited vision we have into the future can be received as a blessing, for it relieves us of the burden of trying to foresee all ends. "Who can bring people to see what will be after them?" (Eccl. 3:22b). If our work serves the times we can foresee, then it is a gift from God.

At this point, we get two more glimpses of God's character. First, God is awesome, eternal, and omniscient, "so that all should stand in awe before him" (Eccl. 3:14). Although we are limited by the conditions of life "under the sun," God is not. There is far more to God than what is apparent to us. This transcendence of God appears again in Ecclesiastes 7:13–14 and 8:12–13.

The next glimpse shows us that God is a God of justice. "God seeks out what has gone by" (Eccl. 3:15), and "God will judge the righteous and the wicked" (Eccl. 3:17). We may suffer oppression, but in time God will set everything right. This idea is repeated later in Ecclesiastes 8:13, 11:9, and 12:14. Many do not experience God's justice in the prevailing unfairness of their circumstances, but the Teacher assures us that our deepest human longings will be fulfilled. God's justice will ultimately come to pass.

Despite this somewhat hopeful note, the exploration of timing ends with a double repetition of "a chasing after wind," once in Ecclesiastes 4:4 (as discussed above) and again in 4:6. Good timing is a blessing, but we do not possess the ability to bring permanent meaning to our lives by means of being in the right place at the right time, no matter how skilled we may be at it.

Food for Thought

Why do you think our limited vision might be experienced as a blessing when it comes to well-timed action? What consolation is there for us in our lives "under the sun," through the glimpses of God's character noted by the Teacher?

_____

_____

_____

_____

_____

_____

_____

_____

Prayer

Pause for a few moments of silence to reflect on this lesson. Then offer a prayer, either spontaneous or by using the following:

Lord,

In the midst of our daily rounds of life, grant that we might see more and more of who you are and find contentment in timing our work to provide blessing to others, at least as far as we are able to imagine.

Amen.

Lesson #4: Friendship and Joy

Friendship (Ecclesiastes 4:7–4:16)

In the Teacher's search for meaning, he turns next to relationships. He especially values friendships in work or "toil." "Two are better than one, because they have a good reward for their toil" (Eccl. 4:9).

David Bowden and Miles Corbett launched their business knowing they needed each other. They own Transition Associates, based in the United Kingdom, which delivers e-learning programs for some of the world's leading corporations.

Miles says, "Maybe I'm the person who creates some vision and direction and gets out there and evangelizes our message, and David's the guy who really runs the business. He's the guy who really sits behind the wheel and says, 'This is how we can achieve it,' or 'No, we can't do that.' But it's a balance." (Learn more of their story at https://vimeo.com/66351541.)

Given the time we spend at work, it's not unusual to find our closest friendships in the workplace. Real friendship and camaraderie at work can keep us working even if we don't need the pay, and even if the work itself doesn't interest us. It's a reason many people find retirement disappointing. We miss our workplace friends after we leave, and we find it difficult to form deep, new friendships without the common goals and adventures in achieving them that brought us together with colleagues at work.

 *Food for Thought*

Has this been true for you in your work experience? If so, what advantages have you found through friendship and camaraderie in your workplace? If this is not yet your experience, what have you seen in the lives of others through their workplace friendships?

_____

_____

_____

_____

_____

_____

Friendships also require openness and a desire to learn from others. The Teacher advises, "Better is a poor but wise youth than an old but foolish king, who will no longer take advice" (Eccl. 4:13), because arrogance and power are often barriers to developing the relationships on which effective work depends (Eccl. 4:14–16). We become friends at work partly because it takes teamwork to do the work well, which is why many people are better at forming friendships at work than in other settings where there is no shared goal.

While the Teacher's exploration of friendship is upbeat, work friendships prove necessarily temporary. Job assignments change, teams are formed and dissolve, colleagues advance or quit, retire or get fired, and new workers join whom we may not like. The Teacher likens it to a new, young king whose subjects receive him gladly at first, but whose popularity drops as a new generation of youth comes to regard him as just another old king. In the end, neither career advancement nor fame guarantees us permanency of friendships. "Surely this also is vanity and a chasing after wind" (Eccl. 4:16).

 Food for Thought

Share a story of collegial work that bound the participants in real friendship. What was the glue that made for such sincere bonding? How does this affect the way you approach your relationships at work?

_____

_____

_____

_____

_____

_____

_____

Joy (Ecclesiastes 5:1–6:9)

The Teacher's search for meaning in work ends with many short lessons that have direct application to our own toil.

1. Listening is wiser than speaking, "therefore let your words be few" (Eccl. 5:1).

2. Keep your promises, above all to God (Eccl. 5:4).

3. Expect the government to be corrupt. Although this is
    not good, it is universal, and it is better than anarchy
    (Eccl. 5:8–9).

4. Obsession for wealth is an addiction, and like any other
    addiction, it consumes those it afflicts (Eccl. 5:10–12), yet
    it does not satisfy (Eccl. 6:7–8).

5. Wealth is fleeting. It may disappear in this life, and it
    is sure to disappear at death. Don't build your life on it
    (Eccl. 5:13–17).

The Teacher explores again the gift of God in allowing us to enjoy
our work and the wealth, possessions, and honor it may bring for
a time. "It is fitting to eat and drink and find enjoyment in all the
toil with which one toils under the sun the few days of the life God
gives us" (Eccl. 5:18).

Although enjoyment is fleeting, it is nonetheless real. "For they
will scarcely brood over the days of their lives, because God
keeps them occupied with the joy of their hearts" (Eccl. 5:20).
Joy comes not from striving more successfully than others, but
from receiving life and work as a gift from God. If joy in our work
does not come as a gift from God, then it does not come at all
(Eccl. 6:1–6).

The Teacher's tone is relatively positive in this section. Yet the
final result is still frustration. For we see plainly that all lives end
in the grave, when the life lived wisely comes to nothing greater
than the life lived foolishly. It is better to look life in the face than
to try to live in a fantasyland. "Better is the sight of the eyes than
the wandering of desire" (Eccl. 6:8a), and so even this quest for
joy is "vanity and a chasing after wind" (Eccl. 6:9).

 *Food for Thought*

After considering the short lessons of the Teacher, what do you see as the most severe disappointments you experience at work? What does the Teacher suggest is the best way to deal with these?

_____

_____

_____

_____

_____

_____

_____

_____

Prayer

Pause for a few moments of silence to reflect on this lesson. Then offer a prayer, either spontaneous or by using the following:

Lord,

More and more, the Teacher makes us face up to the hardships of life in a fallen world, a life "under the sun." Help us to remember you, Lord, in your eternal dwelling place. Please help us to know and appreciate the blessings you have provided to carry us through whatever brokenness we experience in the toil of our days.

Amen.

Chapter 3

No Way to Find Out
What Is Good to Do

(Ecclesiastes 6–8)

Lesson #1: The Ultimate Results of Our Actions
(Ecclesiastes 7:1–14)

The Teacher's exploration so far leads him to believe that a life of
toil amounts to a chasing after wind, for the results of work are not
permanent in the world. So he embarks upon a new quest: To find
out what is best to do with the time he has, without worrying about
how long what he does will last. As with our previous chapters,
this next section has lessons marked by a repetitive concluding
phrase that conveys the Teacher's frustration: "Not find out," or
its equivalent rhetorical question, "Who can find out?"

Graveyards, like old group photographs, hold important lessons
for us. In the film *Dead Poet's Society*, Mr. Keating exhorts his
senior high school class to look carefully at the century-old alumni
pictures and grasp the fact that all the people in them are "pushing
up daises now." It ought to motivate them, he says, to seize the day.

For the same reason, Ecclesiastes recommends that we spend
some serious time in the cemetery (Eccl. 7:1–6). Some people
whistle past the graveyard, refusing to consider its lessons. Their
laughter is like the crackling of burning thorns, as they are con-
sumed in the flames (Eccl. 7:6).

 *Food for Thought*

Describe thoughts you have taken to heart from visiting a grave-yard. What were the ages of the people on the headstones? What does that imply? What is the point of considering the brevity of the lives that went before us?

_____

_____

_____

_____

_____

_____

_____

_____

We cannot foresee out what impact we may have on the world. We cannot even find out why today is different from yesterday (Eccl. 7:10), let alone what tomorrow may bring. It makes sense to enjoy whatever good comes of our toil while we live, but we have no promise that the final end is good, for God "has made the one as well as the other, so that mortals may not find out anything that will come after them" (Eccl. 7:14).

Our ignorance of our legacy has an important implication: good ends are no justification for evil means. For we cannot see the ends of all the actions we take, and as our newspapers report so frequently, it is likely we will be called to account for our evil actions before we die. Politicians who appease public opinion now at the cost of public harm later, financial officers who hide losses this quarter in the hope of making it up next quarter, graduates who lie on a job application with the hope of succeeding in jobs for which they are not qualified—all of them count on futures they cannot bring about. Meanwhile, they cause injustices now that can never truly be erased even if their hopes are realized.

 Food for Thought

What do you hope might be your legacy in your work? How true do you find the Teacher's words in regard to the limitations of your ability to ensure that legacy? What story could you tell to illustrate the problem of evil means to achieve an intended good result?

_____

_____

_____

_____

_____

_____

_____

_____

Prayer

Pause for a few moments of silence to reflect on this lesson. Then offer a prayer, either spontaneous or by using the following:

Lord,

We are all tempted to think we know more than we do and see more than we really see. Please help us to temper the decision making in our workplaces with the humility of knowing we can't know the outcome of whatever we are promoting. Help us guard our hearts from pursuing intended good ends through means of deceit, violence, manipulation, fraud, bribery, pretense, and the many other manifestations of evil.

Amen.

Lesson #2: Good and Evil (Ecclesiastes 7:15–28)

After proclaiming the error of using evil in the pursuit of good, the Teacher exhorts us to act only according to the good. Yet because of our limited vision, the Teacher realizes we cannot know whether any action we take is wholly good or wholly evil. When we imagine we are acting righteously, wickedness may creep in, and vice versa (Eccl. 7:16–18). For "surely there is no one on earth so righteous as to do good without ever sinning" (Eccl. 7:20). The truth of good and evil "is far off, and deep, very deep; who can find it out?" (Eccl. 7:24). As if to emphasize this difficulty, he repeats the characteristic phrase "not found" (Eccl. 7:28).

The best we can do is to fear God (Eccl. 7:18), which means to shun hubris, avoid arrogance, and flee self-righteousness. "God made human beings straightforward, but they have devised many schemes" (Eccl. 7:29). A good self-diagnostic is to examine whether we resort to twisted logic and complicated schemes to justify our actions. Because work has many complexities, multiple objectives, and many factors to be taken into account, moral certainty is usually not possible. But if explaining the ethics of our decision making requires logic as twisted as a pretzel, then we should probably take it as a clue that we are straying into evil territory.

 Food for Thought

Since 2012, there have been an alarming number of auto recalls, notably by car makers Toyota, General Motors, and Volkswagen. To what extent do you think they support the Teacher's point? If you think they do, explain where you think their decision making may have gone wrong.

_____

_____

_____

_____

_____

_____

_____

Lesson #3: Power and Justice (Ecclesiastes 8:1–17)

Politics, government, and the exercise of power are facts of life, and we have a duty to obey those in authority over us, including in our workplaces (Eccl. 8:2–5). Yet we do not know whether the current powers will use their authority justly. Quite possibly, they will use their power selfishly and harm others (Eccl. 8:9). Justice is frequently perverted: the righteous are punished, and the wicked are rewarded (Eccl. 8:10–14).

In the midst of political uncertainty, even at work, the best we can do is to fear God (Eccl. 8:13) and appreciate the opportunities for happiness he gives us. "I commend enjoyment, for there is nothing better for people under the sun than to eat, and drink, and enjoy themselves, for this will go with them in their toil through the days of life that God gives them under the sun" (Eccl. 8:15).

In Ecclesiastes 8:17, "not find out" is repeated three times: "No one can find out what is happening under the sun. However much they may toil in seeking, they will not find it out; even though those who are wise claim to know, they cannot find it out."

This brings to an end the Teacher's search to find out "what is good to do" with the limited time he had. Although he discovered some good practices, the overall result is that he could not find out what was truly meaningful or certain to do lasting good.

Prayer

Pause for a few moments of silence to reflect on this lesson. Then offer a prayer, either spontaneous or by using the following:

> *Lord,*
>
> *We find it hard to believe our lives are so limited in doing good. Please help us to walk humbly in our work and to clarify the complex—to ourselves and to others—so that we do what is best for all those who may be affected by our work. Help us to endure the ups and downs of politics in our workplaces and appreciate the enjoyment you provide every day.*
>
> *Amen.*

Chapter 4

No Way to Know What Comes Afterwards

(Ecclesiastes 9–12)

Now the Teacher explores what comes after this life, in case it might shed light on what is best for now. So he seeks for knowledge about death (Eccl. 9:1–6), Sheol (Eccl. 9:7–10), the time of death (Eccl. 9:11–12), what comes after death (Eccl. 9:13–10:15), the evil that might come after death (Eccl. 10:16–11:2), and the good that might come (Eccl. 11:3–6). Again, the phrases "do not know" and "no knowledge" divide the material into sections. The Teacher finds that it is simply not possible to know what lies ahead.

The dead know nothing. (Eccl. 9:5)

There is no work or thought or knowledge or wisdom in Sheol, to which you are going. (Eccl. 9:10)

Man does not know his time. . . . The sons of men are ensnared at an evil time when it suddenly falls on them. (Eccl. 9:12 NASB)

No one knows what is to happen, and who can tell anyone what the future holds? (Eccl. 10:14)

You do not know what disaster may happen on earth. (Eccl. 11:2)

You do not know which will prosper, this or that, or whether both alike will be good. (Eccl. 11:5–6)

Despite our colossal ignorance about the future, however, the Teacher finds some things that are good to do while we have the chance. We will explore only those passages particularly relevant to work.

 Food for Thought

How does it affect your approach to your work or your career path to consider that you do not know when your time to leave this earth will come? Will your work only be worthwhile if you accomplish a far-off goal before you die, or are you doing anything with lasting value already?

_____

_____

_____

_____

_____

_____

_____

_____

Lesson #1: Throw Yourself into Your Work Wholeheartedly (Ecclesiastes 9:10)

Ken Done wakes in the night with ideas he can't wait to try out. He even paints on his dining room table. While Ken and his wife Judy are both past what some call "retirement age," they have over one hundred employees working for The Ken Done Group of Companies based in Sydney, Australia. The following interview captures his wholehearted approach to his work:

> KEN: I'm 62. I've got not enough time left to worry about anything else other than trying to be a good painter. That's all that interests me, really. And it's one of those things that maybe in your 60s or 70s is when you're at your most productive. You have to get the best out of every day. If you live this day well, then the memories that you have of this day are great and the expectation that you have of the next day is great.
>
> HATTIE: When you wake up in the morning, first thoughts?
>
> KEN: I'm ready to go to work. When I woke up this morning, I said to Judy, "I'm into the studio." I wanted to go in and work. I wanted to work this morning. I want to work every day. I want to play every day.
>
> INTERVIEWER: You're having fun.
>
> KEN: Absolutely. That's how it should be.
>
> (For more of Ken Done's story "Live, Breathe, Eat, Sleep Your Work," visit https://vimeo.com/66352103.)

"Whatever your hand finds to do, do with your might; for there is no work or thought or knowledge or wisdom in Sheol, to which you are going" (Eccl. 9:10). Although we cannot know the final result of our work, we shouldn't let that paralyze us. Humans are created to work (Gen. 2:15), we need to work to survive, and so we might as well work with gusto. The same goes for enjoying the fruits of our labor, whatever they may be. "Eat your bread with enjoyment, and drink your wine with a merry heart; for God has long ago approved what you do" (Eccl. 9:7).

 *Food for Thought*

How sensible do you find this as a strategy to deal with your working life? What would have to change for you to be able to adopt this attitude to both your way of working and the enjoyment of the fruits of your work?

_____

_____

_____

_____

_____

_____

_____

_____

Accept Success and Failure as a Part of Life (Ecclesiastes 9:11–12)

> I saw that under the sun the race is not to the swift, nor the battle to the strong, nor bread to the wise, nor riches to the intelligent, nor favor to the skillful; but time and chance happen to them all. (Eccl. 9:11)

This was a key theme of the 1995 movie *Forrest Gump*, in which an intellectually challenged boy from Mississippi grows up through the tumultuous post World War II years of the late 1940s, and we watch his life unfold through more than four decades to the early 1990s. His intellectual simplicity made him immune to the sophistry of the popular culture, and that—alongside plain good luck—kept him from the tragedies and failures experienced by the people close to him as well as the political leaders of his day.

Success or failure may indeed be due to dumb luck. This is not to say that hard work and ingenuity aren't important. They prepare us to make the most of the chances of life, and they may create opportunities that otherwise wouldn't exist. Yet one who succeeds at work may be no more deserving than another who fails.

For example, Microsoft had a crack at success largely because of IBM's offhand decision to use the MS-DOS operating system for a backwater project called the personal computer. Bill Gates later reflected, "Our timing in setting up the first software company aimed at personal computers was essential to our success. The timing wasn't entirely luck, but without great luck it couldn't have happened."

 Food for Thought

What is the role of luck in your successes and failures? When has your work left you prepared you to make the most of fortunate circumstances? Are there times when a lack of preparedness has contributed to problems you have been tempted to blame on others?

_____

_____

_____

_____

_____

_____

_____

Prayer

Pause for a few moments of silence to reflect on this lesson. Then offer a prayer, either spontaneous or by using the following:

Lord,

How hard it is to acknowledge our smallness, the sense of unknowing that can come over us at a funeral service, or the mystery of the "why" of our circumstances. Thank you for confronting us with our dependence on wisdom from above, since we cannot find the answers by simply observing life under the sun.

Amen.

Lesson #2: Work Diligently and Invest Wisely (Ecclesiastes 10:18–11:6)

Ecclesiastes 10:18–11:6 contains the most direct financial advice to be found anywhere in the Bible. First, be diligent; otherwise your household economy will collapse like a leaky, rotten roof (Eccl. 10:18).

Second, financial well-being matters: "Money meets every need" (Eccl. 10:19). This doesn't mean that money is *all* that matters. But it is a plain fact that money is a daily essential for purchasing food, transportation, medicine, repairs, tools, or a child's tuition. We need money for vacations, even funerals. Almost everything we need to sustain our mortal lives requires money, which is therefore necessary and good for meeting human need.

Third, be careful about people in authority. "Do not curse the king, even in your thoughts, or curse the rich, even in your bedroom; for a bird of the air may carry your voice, or some winged creature tell the matter" (Eccl. 10:20). This is especially urgent to grasp in the age of social media. When you disparage your boss or belittle a customer, the record of it and the complaints against you remain digitally archived and accessible, ad infinitum.

Fourth, diversify your investments (Eccl. 11:1–2). The proverb "Send out your bread upon the waters" refers to investments; the waters represent a venture in overseas trading. Thus giving portions to "seven or eight" refers to diverse investments, "for you do not know what disaster may happen on earth" (Eccl. 11:2).

 Food for Thought

What is your attitude toward money, and how might it change in the light of these four points of advice from the Teacher?

_____

_____

_____

_____

_____

_____

Fifth, don't be overly timid about investing (Eccl. 11:3–5). What will happen will happen, and we cannot control that (Eccl. 11:3). We should find the courage to take reasonable risks. "Whoever observes the wind will not plant; whoever regards the clouds will not reap" (Eccl. 11:4). If this seems almost like a contradiction of Ecclesiastes 11:1–2, remember that the Teacher is struggling with the problem that he "can't find out" what is truly best.

Sixth, understand that success is in God's hands. Since we don't know what plans or purposes God has for us, we should not be so silly as to second-guess him (Eccl. 11:5).

Seventh, be persistent (Eccl. 11:6). Don't work hard for a little while and then say, "I tried that, and it didn't work." When a venture is well conceived, keep at it!

The Teacher's search for knowledge about the future ends at Ecclesiastes 11:5–6 with a triple repetition of the marker phrase "not know." This reminds us that although working wholeheartedly, accepting success and failure as part of life, and working diligently and investing wisely are good practices, they are adaptations to deal with our ignorance of the future. If we truly knew how our actions would play out, then we could plan confidently for success. If we knew which investments would turn out well, then we wouldn't need to diversify as a hedge against systemic losses.

It is hard to know whether to hang our heads in sorrow for the disasters that happen to us in this fallen world, or to praise God that it is still possible to muddle through and maybe even to do well in such a world. Or is the truth a bit of both?

 Food for Thought

Has the Teacher convinced you that we cannot know what lies in the future? If so, does this suggest changes you should make in the way you go about your work?

_____

_____

_____

_____

_____

_____

_____

_____

Prayer

Pause for a few moments of silence to reflect on this lesson. Then offer a prayer, either spontaneous or by using the following:

Lord,

The drumbeat of the Teacher has been that most human effort is vain—chasing the wind. Since we can't know what is to come, help us enjoy what you have given us to do and whatever fruit that produces now. Open our hearts to hear what you have revealed of the life that is to come.

Amen.

Lesson #3: The Conclusion of Ecclesiastes

A Poem on Youth and Old Age (Ecclesiastes 11:7–12:8)

Given the bracing lessons of this book, it is appropriate that the Teacher concludes with a poem exhorting the young to good cheer (Eccl. 11:7–12:1)—but not to lose sight of the Creator. In a poem remarkably beautiful, even as an English translation from the original Hebrew, he also recounts the downward spiral from the vigor of youth to the frailty of old age (Eccl. 12:2–8). "The silver cord is snapped, the golden bowl is broken, and the pitcher is broken at the fountain" (Eccl. 12:6).

In this soulful way, he completes the pattern found in the earlier chapters of the book. Yes, there is much good to be found in our life and work. But ultimately it goes by quickly—like a breath. The Teacher closes as he began, "Vanity of vanities, says the Teacher; all is vanity" (Eccl. 12:8).

Narrator's Epilogue: Praise for the Teacher (Ecclesiastes 12:9–14)

The final chapter of the book is an epilogue by a new voice—the narrator or editor of the book—about the Teacher. It praises the Teacher's wisdom and repeats his admonition to fear God.

But the narrator brings forward new elements not mentioned earlier by the Teacher—namely, the wisdom of following God's commandments in light of God's future judgment. "The end of the matter; all has been heard. Fear God, and keep his commandments; for that is the whole duty of everyone. For God will bring every deed into judgment, including every secret thing, whether good or evil" (Eccl. 12:13–14).

God's future judgment is offered as the interpretive key that can help us discern what is precious and what is worthless, so we can sort out the mix of good and evil that pervades our work in this fallen world. The glimpses of God's character we have seen in the book—God's generosity, justice, and transcendence beyond our world bound in time—depict an underlying goodness in the foundations of the world, if only we could live accordingly.

Our future accountability hints that in God's time the tensions so vividly described by the Teacher will be brought into a harmony not visible in the Teacher's day "under the sun."

 *Food for Thought*

Do you think that knowing God's character can give us a good idea of what is worthwhile in our daily life and work? What have you seen of God's character? What of God's character would you like to have more of yourself? Discuss.

_____

_____

_____

_____

_____

_____

_____

Ecclesiastes and the Good News

Unlike the Teacher, followers of Christ today see a concrete hope beyond the fallen world. For we are witnesses to the life, death, and resurrection of a better Teacher, Jesus, whose power did not die with the end of his days under the sun (Luke 23:44). What the writer of Ecclesiastes could not know—as he was so keenly aware—is that God would send his Son not to condemn the world but to restore the world to the way God intended it to be (John 3:17). So, the days of life broken "under the sun" are passing in favor of the kingdom of God on earth, where God's people "need no light of lamp or sun, for the Lord God will be their light" (Rev. 22:5). Because of this, the world in which we live is not only the remnant of the fallen world, but also the vanguard of the kingdom of Christ "coming down out of heaven from God" (Rev. 21:2).

The work we do as followers of Christ therefore does—or at least could—have eternal value that the Teacher could not see or know. In a sense, we are able to live both "under the sun" in a broken world *and* in the kingdom of God that is coming. This allows us to appreciate Ecclesiastes as God's gift to us as it stands. For we also live daily life under much the same conditions the Teacher did. As Paul reminds us:

> We know that the whole creation has been groaning in labor pains until now; and not only the creation, but we ourselves, who have the first fruits of the Spirit, groan inwardly while we wait for adoption, the redemption of our bodies. (Rom. 8:22–23)

 Food for Thought

What do you think it means to live in the tension of life under the sun *and* in the kingdom of God? In what new ways does your awareness of Christ and his kingdom allow you to make your working life under the sun more meaningful?

_____

_____

_____

_____

_____

_____

_____

_____

Prayer

Pause for a few moments of silence to reflect on this lesson. Then offer a prayer, either spontaneous or by using the following:

Lord,

It is true that we prefer to hide from pain and suffering. It is true that we are good at avoiding the challenges that life under the sun and life in Christ place on us. Grant that we take from this remarkable book a renewed willingness to look life in the face with boldness and hope by the power of your Spirit.

Amen.

Chapter 5

Song of Songs and Work

(Song of Songs 1–2)

Lesson #1: Introduction to Song of Songs

Song of Songs, also known as the Song of Solomon, is love poetry. Yet it is also a profound depiction of the meaning, value, and beauty of work. The Song sings of lovers who court, marry, and then labor together in an ideal picture of life, family, and work. We will explore themes of beauty, diligence, hardship, pleasure, passion, family, and joy as depicted in the wide variety of work seen in the Song of Songs.

Please note that while this book celebrates an integration of marriage and work, in no way does it make singleness a second-class lifestyle. In the context of the book's historical period, marriage was generally an economic necessity, which is clearly not the same in the urban work of the twenty-first century.

 Food for Thought

If you have read the Song of Songs before, what are your initial thoughts on it? What meaning or meanings have you found in it?

_____

_____

_____

_____

_____

_____

_____

_____

In the ancient world, all poetry was sung, and the Song is no exception as it is lyrics to a song collection. It would have been performed by singers consisting of male and female leads with a chorus. Song of Songs should probably be thought of as a concert piece created for an aristocratic audience in Solomon's court.

Food for Thought

If you are studying this poem in a group, try reading it in its parts with male and female leads, with others joining in as the chorus. How does this help you hear the various themes throughout?

_____

_____

_____

_____

_____

_____

_____

Song of Songs has strong analogies to the love music of ancient Egypt composed centuries earlier, which was also meant for aristocratic audiences. The lyrics of Egyptian poetry, although in many ways similar to the Song of Songs, are rather lighthearted and often focus on the ecstasy and afflictions of young lovers. Unlike them, however, the Song of Songs is profound and theological, provoking serious thoughts on love and even work.

Although there are numerous interpretations of the Song of Songs, we will approach this book as a collection of songs that center on the love of a man and a woman. This is the plain sense of the text and the most fruitful way to explore meanings in the text. This is love poetry that celebrates the beauty of a wedding and the joy of love.

 Food for Thought

Make a note of the places in the poem that provide glimpses of God. Before we begin the study, what do you imagine it has to say about work?

_____

_____

_____

_____

_____

_____

_____

Prayer

Pause for a few moments of silence to reflect on this lesson. Then offer a prayer, either spontaneous or by using the following:

> *Lord,*
>
> *We thank you for the breadth and scope of the Scriptures that touch our humanity. Grant as we explore this remarkable love poem that we can learn more truly what it means to celebrate beauty, diligence, hardship, pleasure, passion, family, and joy in the work you have given us.*
>
> *Amen.*

Lesson #2: The Hardship and the Beauty of Work (Song of Songs 1:1–8)

The Song begins with the woman speaking of her love, but she also speaks of how her skin has been darkened because her brothers made her work the family vineyard (Song 1:6). By the sixth verse in this song about love, we are already reading about work. In the ancient world, people disdained dark skin, not for racial reasons but for reasons of class and economics. Dark (tanned) skin signified someone who labored out in the fields in the sun, whereas untanned skin signified someone of wealth or ranking and was especially prized as a mark of beauty in women.

The woman in our poem, however, has a beauty that transcends her tanned appearance and her outdoor work: "I am very dark, but lovely" (Song 1:5). Furthermore, her job prepares her for the future, when she will tend her own vineyard (Song 8:12). And so we immediately discover a woman who works with her hands and, contrary to cultural expectations, she is beautiful and worthy of praise.

Food for Thought

Do the requirements of your work conflict with your desire to be beautiful or healthy? Does this affect men differently from women in your occupation or workplace? If so, what could be done about it?

_____

_____

_____

_____

_____

_____

_____

The beauty of work and working people is often obscured by competing notions of beauty. The ancient Greek world, whose thought still influences contemporary culture, regarded work as the enemy of beauty. But the biblical perspective is that work actually has an intrinsic beauty.

Solomon builds himself a palanquin (a seat carried on poles), and the Song extols the beauty of the artistry behind it. It is literally a labor of love (Song 3:10). He puts its beauty to use in the service of love—transporting his beloved to their wedding (Song 3:11)—yet the work is already beautiful in its own right. Work is not only a means to an end, but also a source of aesthetic creativity. Believers are encouraged to praise the beauty in others' work, including the work of their spouses.

As a demonstration that beauty can be found even in occupations typically regarded as un-aesthetic, watch this short trailer on the documentary film *Trash Dance* (https://www.youtube.com/watch?v=eiW—U3UxLE) where drivers of trash trucks participate in a choreographed demonstration of their work, set to music on an old airfield in Austin, Texas.

 Food for Thought

Describe the beauty you find in your own work. Do you attempt to create beauty in your work? Would others value it? Would it make you less productive or otherwise interfere with your work, or would it improve the value of your work?

_____

_____

_____

_____

_____

_____

_____

_____

Relationship and Work (Song of Songs 1:7–8)

In Song 1:7–8, the woman seeks her beloved, whom she regards as the finest of men. Her friends tell her that the obvious place to find him is at his work, where he is tending the sheep. Nothing about his work prohibits her presence. In this poetic cameo, there is nothing like our modern notion that time on the job belongs to the employer, while time off belongs to the family.

Much contemporary work makes family interaction while working impossible. For obvious safety reasons, truck drivers shouldn't text their families while on the road, and lawyers shouldn't answer a phone call from their spouses during closing arguments. Still, there is a separation between work and family today that didn't exist in earlier times. This separation began in the 1800s in the West with the Industrial Revolution when various forms of work moved away from homes and into factories or offices. This distinction between workplace and family place seems to be diminishing in many parts of the world as more people now work from home.

 Food for Thought

To what extent is the industry in which you work accessible to your family or friends? If you are able to work from home, do you find it to be a good thing?

_____

_____

_____

_____

_____

_____

_____

Prayer

Pause for a few moments of silence to reflect on this lesson. Then offer a prayer, either spontaneous or by using the following:

Lord,

Often we bury the beauty of our work beneath the distorted notions of value we find around us. Help us to celebrate and enjoy the creativity in our particular tasks and to encourage others in the same way. Help us to be accessible to those who love us or depend on us, even as we work.

Amen.

Lesson #3: When Work Is a Pleasure (Song of Songs 1:9–2:17)

In Song of Songs 1:9–2:7, the man and woman sing of their devotion to each other. He speaks of how beautiful she is, and she proclaims how happy she is in love. Then they sing of the glories of the arrival of springtime, and he invites her to come away with him (Song 2:8–17). This is in the context of the agricultural economy of ancient Israel, and a trip into the countryside in springtime is not just a picnic. It involves work.

Pruning is necessary to ensure a good harvest ("the time of singing" can also be translated "the time of pruning," Song 2:12–13 NASB). In addition, Song 2:15 says that foxes, animals that love to eat young grapes, have to be kept from the vineyards lest they spoil the harvest.

But the man and woman have light hearts. They turn this task into a game, chasing away the "little foxes." Their work is so amenable to games of love that it leads to the double entendre, "our vineyards are in blossom." This glorious picture of agricultural life in springtime hearkens back to the Garden of Eden, where tending the plants was meant to be a pleasure.

One contemporary application of this is where elementary school teachers involve children in basic chores, such as cleaning up the schoolyard, but they turn the chore into a game. In Australia, the children play "Emu Parade," where they pretend they are foraging emus; when in reality, they are competing with other children in picking up the most litter!

 Food for Thought

In what way can you relate this rural picture to your own situation? What kind of activities in your work allows for the possibility of both work and play?

_____

_____

_____

_____

_____

_____

Genesis 3:17–19 tells us that because of sin labor has become tinged with drudgery. But this is not the original or proper meaning of work. This episode in the Song is a glimpse of how God desires life to be for us, almost as if sin had never happened. It is as if Isaiah 65:21 were already fulfilled: "They shall build houses and inhabit them; they shall plant vineyards and eat their fruit." The kingdom of God does not eliminate work, but rather restores the joy and delightful relationships in work. (See *Revelation* in The Theology of Work Bible and Your Work study series for more on work in the ultimate kingdom of God.)

 *Food for Thought*

Consider all those tasks you wish you could avoid or skip. How much of it do you consider drudgery? What are some creative ways you could make these tasks more meaningful and maybe even an enjoyable part of your day? What aspects of drudgery do you simply have to live with, and how could you be thankful in your work anyway?

_____

_____

_____

_____

_____

_____

_____

_____

Prayer

Pause for a few moments of silence to reflect on this lesson. Then offer a prayer, either spontaneous or by using the following:

Lord,

There are many obstacles in our work life that sabotage enjoyment of the work you have given us to do. Please help us find the joy in our tasks and make this joy infectious in our workplaces. Help us overcome the effects of sinful attitudes that are so destructive to our enjoyment of work.

Amen.

Chapter 6

Passion, Family, and Work

(Song of Songs 3–8)

Lesson #1 Celebration of Love, Sex, and Work

A series of songs now describes the marriage of the man and woman and their coming together. The woman yearns for the man (Song 3:1–5), and then she comes to him on a lovely palanquin (3:6–11). The man, wearing a crown, receives her (3:11). In an Israelite wedding, the bride arrived in a sedan surrounded by attendants (3:7), and she was received by her groom, who wore a crown. Song 3:11 confirms that this text celebrates the day of his wedding.

The man sings of his love for his bride (Song 4:1–15), and their wedding night is described in vivid images and metaphors (4:16–5:8). The woman then sings of her love for her beloved (5:9–6:3), followed by him singing about her beauty (6:4–9). The couple then sing of their love for each other (6:10–8:4).

 Food for Thought

In the scenes of this marriage, what do the images presented here mean to you? What do you think they conveyed in that ancient culture?

_____

_____

_____

_____

_____

_____

_____

_____

The text is frankly sexual, and Christian preachers and writers have tended to avoid the Song or to allegorize it out of concern it is too racy for polite religious society. But the sex in the text is intentional. A song about the passion between two lovers on their wedding day would be missing something if it failed to mention sex! And the sex is intimately connected to both the household and the work in the Song.

Upon their marriage, the lovers create a household, the primary unit of economic activity in the ancient world. Without sex, it could not be populated with children who grow up to assist and increase the family enterprise. Moreover, passion (including sex) between spouses is the glue holding the household together through the prosperity, adversity, joy, and stress that characterize a family's life and work.

 *Food for Thought*

How does this depiction of mutual delight in each other, of sexual enjoyment in marriage and the creation of a family economic unit, relate to the world in which you live and work? Does your work culture encourage or discourage this possibility?

_____

_____

_____

_____

_____

_____

_____

While many couples report dissatisfaction with the amount of time they have for lovemaking, a major cause is that one or both partners are too busy in their separated work situations. Even in television sitcoms, we see how work can intrude through smartphones into the most intimate settings! Yet the Song of Songs clearly promotes God's design for our lives, in making time for the enjoyment of intimacy and sex with our spouse.

Throughout these verses, we see imagery drawn from landscape of Israel—its agriculture and shepherding. The woman's body is a "garden" (Song 5:1). The man's "cheeks are like beds of spices" (5:13). Enjoying his bride, he is like a man gathering lilies in a garden (6:2). She is awesome like Jerusalem (6:4). Her hair is like a "flock of goats moving down the slopes of Gilead" (6:5). Her "teeth are like a flock of ewes" (6:6). Her stature is like that of a palm tree (7:7). They desire to go to the "vineyards" (7:12). She rouses her beloved "under the apple tree" (8:5). The joy of their love is intimately connected to the world of their work. They express their happiness with images drawn from what they experience in their gardens and flocks—the world of their common work.

 Food for Thought

What effect does your work and the way you go about it have on the people in your household? Does it contribute to their economic stability? Does it promote the intimacy appropriate for your situation? Or does it pull you away from good relationships and perhaps even push you toward unhealthy ones?

_____

_____

_____

_____

_____

_____

_____

Prayer

Pause for a few moments of silence to reflect on this lesson. Then offer a prayer, either spontaneous or by using the following:

> *Lord,*
>
> *We all too easily allow our work and careers to compete with our relationships with those who love us and who need our love. Help us to imagine an integrated life in which our careers and our family relationships are mutually support-ing. Thank you for the Song of Songs with its encourage-ment to enjoy life and work with those you have given us to love and care for, and for the free enjoyment of sex depicted in marriage.*
>
> *Amen.*

Lesson #2: A Family Enterprise

What we have read in the Song so far suggests that sexual fulfill-ment, nurture of family, and work belong together. In the poem, the whole of life is beautifully integrated.

As already mentioned, before the Industrial Revolution, most people worked with family members in the households where they lived, and this remains true in much of the world. While the Song paints an idyllic view of this arrangement, the reality of household-based labor has been marred by limited access to edu-cation, exploitation with grinding toil, humiliation, bonded service, even slavery. (For a fuller treatment on this issue, see *Exodus* in The Bible and Your Work study series.) Yet the Song expresses our most human desire—and God's design—that our work be woven into the tapestry of our relationships, beginning with family.

 *Food for Thought*

True Vine is a microbrewing company in Tyler, Texas, that prioritizes faith, family, and community. Read more about their dreams and work at http://www.bscenemag.com/cover-story/new-year-new-brew. To what extent does True Vine demonstrate the ideal of work/family life we see in the Song of Songs?

_____

_____

_____

_____

_____

_____

_____

In developed economies, despite a trend toward working from home, much work occurs outside the household. In that circumstance it would seem that our urban societies of the twenty-first century miss out on the integration of work with family and other relationships visible in the Song of Songs. And we certainly can't apply its poetry as a call for us all to move to farms and chase away the little foxes!

But it *can* suggest that modern workplaces should not ignore their workers' family lives and needs. Many workplaces provide daycare for workers' children, career development that respects parenting needs, time away for family care needs, and—in countries with private health care—medical insurance for workers' families.

 *Food for Thought*

Bright Horizons, an international company based in Watertown, Massachusetts, focuses on child and family care and is one employer that addresses the issues in our study. Read its company culture webpage (http://www.brighthorizons.com/careers/company-culture) and then explain to what extent it seems to uphold, at least in principle, the Song of Songs' idyll for integrating work with family and other relationships.

_____

_____

_____

_____

_____

_____

_____

_____

Most modern workplaces fall far short of the model of family care we see in the Song. The recent trend toward shifting work from offices to homes may or may not improve matters, depending on how costs, revenues, support services, and risks are distributed. As we develop our workplaces today, perhaps the Song of Songs can invite us to be creative: families could start businesses in which their members can work together; and companies could employ spouses together, or help one spouse find work when relocating the other. Recent decades have seen much innovation and research in this area, both in secular and Christian circles.

 *Food for Thought*

Imagine for a moment that there are no constraints on you and you could create your dream job situation. What would that look like? Would it involve your family and/or friends, colleagues from your current workplace, others?

_____

_____

_____

_____

_____

_____

_____

_____

Prayer

Pause for a few moments of silence to reflect on this lesson. Then offer a prayer, either spontaneous or by using the following:

Lord,

We know that the creative longings you place in our hearts are hints of our being made as your children. Please help us to tease out these longings in regard to our ideal of work so that we might reflect your desire for us to be joyful in our work.

Amen.

Lesson #3: The Joy of Work

Paid/Unpaid Work

The Song of Songs can also heighten our appreciation of unpaid work. In pre-industrial households, there was little distinction between paid and unpaid work, since work occurred in an informal setting that valued all contributions to a household's well-being.

In industrial and post-industrial societies, wage earning to support the household is mostly work done away from the home (though, as we have already noted, that gap is beginning to close). One outcome of this arrangement is that the unpaid work done within the household receives less respect than the paid work done away from it. When money supersedes other contributions to the household, it becomes the measure of work's worth, and sometimes even of an individual's worth.

 Food for Thought

What are the advantages of wage earning away from our homes? And what are the disadvantages? What thoughts do you have on altering the structure to give proper recognition to the unpaid workers of the household?

_____

_____

_____

_____

_____

_____

_____

Homes cannot function without the unpaid work of maintaining the household, raising children, caring for aged and incapacitated family members, and sustaining social and community relationships. It is all the more important to us, then, that the Song of Songs depicts the value of work in terms of its overall benefit to the household, not its monetary contribution. Therefore, the Song can pose a challenge to many churches and those who guide Christians, for it is uncommon for Christians to receive much help from their churches about arranging their work lives. A pressing challenge for churches today is to equip their members for making godly, wise, realistic choices about work in relationship to family and community. Few are equipped for this.

Church leaders rarely have the necessary practical knowledge to help members land jobs or create workplaces that move toward the ideal depicted in the Song. If you want to know how to better integrate your work as a nurse with your family relationships, for example, you probably need to talk more with other nurses than with your pastor. But perhaps churches could do more to help their members recognize God's design for work and relationships, express their hopes and struggles, and join with similar workers to develop viable options.

Food for Thought

If you examine your wage earning and the state of your closest relationships, how well is your monetary reward contributing to the overall health of your family or friendships? If it is not, what is lacking? If there is some concern for you on this issue, to whom will you turn for advice?

_____

_____

_____

_____

_____

_____

_____

Joy (Song of Songs 8:6–14)

And so the Song arrives at its climax: love is sacred and should be protected; it cannot be bought (Song 8:7). The woman compares her love life to tending a vineyard (Song 8:12), asserting that although Solomon may have many vineyards to be tended by his workers (Song 8:11), her joy is in taking care of her own family.

Happiness does not consist in wealth or in having others do your work for you; it consists in working for the benefit of those you love. Love, therefore, is not only expressing our feelings for others, but in doing acts that prove our love.

In its conclusion, the Song of Songs gives us an ideal picture of love and family, life and work. Joy in the shared work of the household is a central feature—almost as though sin had never happened. In the Song's poetry, work has a beauty that is integrated into a wholesome and joyful life, an ideal for which we can strive with all the creativity in us. Labor is meant to be an act of love so that marriage and household relationships find support through work. Although work is an essential element of marriage and family life, it must always serve the most comprehensive action of all: love.

 Food for Thought

As a follow-up to the study on Ecclesiastes, how does the Song of Songs add meaning to the conclusions of the Teacher? In our in-between state of waiting for the completion of the kingdom of God on earth, in what way can you see yourself reflecting the truth found in the Song of Songs in your home and workplace?

_____

_____

_____

_____

_____

_____

_____

Prayer

Pause for a few moments of silence to reflect on this lesson. Then offer a prayer, either spontaneous or by using the following:

> *Lord,*
>
> *How we want to be found faithful stewards in your house-hold of faith! Thank you for the beauty and wonder of the wholeness of life depicted in the Song of Songs. By your Spirit, help us transform our homes, workplaces, and churches so that together we realize your desire for joy in our lives and work.*
>
> *Amen.*

Wisdom for Using This Study in the Workplace

Community within the workplace is a good thing and a Christian community within the workplace is even better. Sensitivity is needed, however, when we get together in the workplace (even a Christian workplace) to enjoy fellowship time together, learn what the Bible has to say about our work, and encourage one another in Jesus' name. When you meet at your place of employment, here are some guidelines to keep in mind:

- *Be sensitive to your surroundings.* Know your company policy about having such a group on company property. Make sure not to give the impression that this is a secret or exclusive group.

- *Be sensitive to time constraints.* Don't go over your allotted time. Don't be late to work! Make sure you are a good witness to the others (especially non-Christians) in your workplace by being fully committed to your work during working hours and doing all your work with excellence.

- *Be sensitive to the shy or silent members of your group.* Encourage everyone in the group and give them a chance to talk.

- *Be sensitive to the others by being prepared.* Read the Bible study material and Scripture passages and think about your answers to the questions ahead of time.

These Bible studies are based on the Theology of Work biblical commentary. Besides reading the commentary, please visit the Theology of Work website (www.theologyofwork.org) for videos, interviews, and other material on the Bible and your work.

Leader's Guide

Living Word. It is always exciting to start a new group and study. The possibilities of growth and relationship are limitless when we engage with one another and with God's word. Always remember that God's word is "alive and active, sharper than any double-edged sword" (Heb. 4:12) and when you study his word, it should change you.

A Way Has Been Made. Please know you and each person joining your study have been prayed for by people you will probably never meet who share your faith. And remember that "the LORD himself goes before you and will be with you; he will never leave you nor forsake you. Do not be afraid; do not be discouraged" (Deut. 31:8). As a leader, you need to know that truth. Remind yourself of it throughout this study.

Pray. It is always a good idea to pray for your study and those involved weeks before you even begin. It is recommended to pray for yourself as leader, your group members, and the time you are about to spend together. It's no small thing you are about to start and the more you prepare in the Spirit, the better. Apart from Jesus, we can do nothing (John 14:5). Remain in him and "you will bear much fruit" (John 15:5). It's also a good idea to have trusted friends pray and intercede for you and your group as you work through the study.

Spiritual Battle. Like it or not, the Bible teaches that we are in the middle of a spiritual battle. The enemy would like nothing more than for this study to be ineffective. It would be part of his scheme to have group members not show up or engage in any discussion. His victory would be that your group just passes time together going through the motions of a yet another Bible study. You, as a leader, are a threat to the enemy, as it is your desire to lead people down the path of righteousness (as taught in Proverbs). Read Ephesians 6:10–20 and put your armor on.

Scripture. Prepare before your study by reading the selected Scripture verses ahead of time.

Chapters. Each chapter contains approximately three lessons. As you work through the lessons, keep in mind the particular chapter theme in connection with the lessons. These lessons are designed so that you can go through them in thirty minutes each.

Lessons. Each lesson has teaching points with their own discussion questions. This format should keep the participants engaged with the text and one another.

Food for Thought. The questions at the end of the teaching points are there to create discussion and deepen the connection between each person and the content being addressed. You know the people in your group and should feel free to come up with your own questions or adapt the ones provided to best meet the needs of your group. Again, this would require some preparation beforehand.

Opening and Closing Prayers. Sometimes prayer prompts are given before and usually after each lesson. These are just suggestions. You know your group and the needs present, so please feel free to pray accordingly.

Bible Commentary. The Theology of Work series contains a variety of books to help you apply the Scriptures and Christian faith to your work. This Bible study is based on the *Theology of Work Bible Commentary,* examining what the Bible say about work. This commentary is intended to assist those with theological training or interest to conduct in-depth research into passages or books of Scripture.

Video Clips. The Theology of Work website (www.theologyofwork .org) provides good video footage of people from the marketplace highlighting the teaching from all the books of the Bible. It would be great to incorporate some of these videos into your teaching time.

Enjoy your study! Remember that God's word does not return void—ever. It produces fruit and succeeds in whatever way God has intended it to succeed.

> "So shall my word be that goes out from my mouth;
>   it shall not return to me empty,
>   but it shall accomplish that which I purpose,
>   and succeed in the thing for which I sent it." (Isa. 55:11)

"This commentary was written exactly for those of us who aim to integrate our faith and work on a daily basis and is an excellent reminder that God hasn't called the world to go to the church, but has called the Church to go to the world."

BONNIE WURZBACHER
FORMER SENIOR VICE PRESIDENT, THE COCA-COLA COMPANY